Pathways

Restful Meditations

Merry Christmas Volney

Love Kevin & Gee

Pathways
Restful Meditations

Zen Haiku translated by Gary Crounse
Photography by Rosalie Blakey Wardell

GIBBS·SMITH
➔P
PUBLISHER

PEREGRINE SMITH BOOKS
SALT LAKE CITY

First Edition
97 96 95 5 4 3 2 1

This is a Peregrine Smith Book, published by
Gibbs Smith, Publisher
P.O. Box 667
Layton, Utah 84041

Design by Randall Smith Associates
Edited by Gail Yngve

Printed and bound in Canada

Library of Congress Cataloging-in-Publication Data
Crounse, Gary.
Pathways: restful meditations /translated by Gary
Crounse :
photographed by Rosalie Blakey Wardell
p. cm.
Haiku written by Kamishiwa Sensei.
ISBN 0–87905–669–X
1. Crounse, Gary–Translations into English.
I. Wardell, Rosalie Blakey. II. Title
PL847.5.R76L43 1995
895.6'15–dc20
                                        94-41882
                                        CIP

Translator's Note

Writing a poem to accompany a painting is a popular literary form in China and Japan. The same arrangement is in place here, with the difference that the painting is a photograph.

These poems and images with their commentaries constitute a cycle of leaving and returning home—a complete turn of the wheel. The parallel themes of home and away, coming and going, having and being are viewed from several perspectives. When at the end, leaving home becomes returning home, the traveler/reader returns to the starting place–where, in fact, he/she always was. It is a rambling pilgrimage on a stationary bicycle.

Once when Lao-Tzu and a companion were out walking, they spotted the distant towers of the city that was their destination. Lao-Tzu's friend began to quicken his pace in anticipation, but Lao-Tzu refused to be rushed, explaining, "Here, too, it is good."

Here is the beginning—
Just step upon the stone,
Along the path with others,
Yet essentially alone.

*In the beginning, we enter the path
alone. Later, we recognize others on the
same road, but even so, each is
responsible for his or her own progress.*

Leaving friends and family
To wander twisting roads,
Weathered and still at last—
Everywhere at home.

*When someone commits to the life of a
monk, the person is said to "leave
home." It means leaving everything
that is familiar and taking up a life of
hard discipline.*

Squinting at the stranger,
While perched along the wall,
'Who's that,' they ask—
'One of those upstart humans?'

Even the lowly pigeon looks down the
centuries at the newcomers and is
intrigued by their lively cavorting.
These bipedal apes are really something.

Working together in silence,
Hour after hour.
Without even trying–
Camaraderie.

It may be that the strongest bonds are forged in silence. In a Zen monastery, monks work side by side for hours without ever speaking. Yet the sense of fraternity grows steadily without the aid of conversation.

Little circles of shade
Faithfully follow along,
Heaven's overarching sphere—
We generously belong.

We may not always notice, but each of us carries around an interior reflection of heaven all the time. The poet points out that we all enjoy the shade of heaven's broad protection—individually and together.

Guardians of the gate,
Ferocious Kings of Light,
Behind the fearsome snarl—
An almost motherly might.

In Buddhism, the protective deities are always depicted as threatening and ferocious. However, it is good to remember that as they stand at the four corners of the world, they are securing for us a place to bow. In other words, the whole universe becomes a sanctuary where it is safe to lay down one's defenses, a place where we are free to open up.

Daruma plucked his eyelids,
The first to harvest tea.
After nine years steeping in
darkness—Bowls of clarity.

*In a legend about Daruma
(Bodhidharma) while he meditated, he
was distracted by persistent drowsiness.
In order to keep his eyes from growing
heavy, he plucked off his eyelids. Where
they landed on the ground, the first tea
bushes grew. Ever since, monks have
used tea as a way of preserving alertness
in their meditation.*

*The "nine years steeping" refers to the
well-known story about Daruma, who
spent that length of time meditating in
a cave before he was ready to emerge
and teach others.*

Strange how a teapot
Can represent at the same time
The comforts of solitude
And the pleasures of company.

When the mind is bright and still, there is something that is constant. Sitting alone in a quiet reverie, there's a knock at the door. Without a moment's hesitation, "Come in, come in. Have a cup of tea." Your privacy extends to include the whole world. Chuang-Tzu said if you want to find perfect security, you must hide the world in the world so that nothing can get away.

Mountain floating on water,
Stillness over the lake.
The superior man reins in his anger
And dedicates himself to restraint.

*The forty-first hexagram of the I Ching
is Mountain over the Lake. The theme
is stillness and restraint.*

A grove of stately pines
Shivering in the wind,
Upright, ancient thoughts—
Unwillingness to bend.

*In Asian symbolism, the pine represents
steadfastness and timelessness since it
remains green even in winter. The poet
suggests that, carried to an extreme,
steadfastness can become rigidity of
thought and petrifaction of the heart.*

Jizo descending into hell
To save the ones condemned,
His shiny pate reflects
The flaming hells within.

Jizo Bosatsu, or Kshitigarbha Bodhisattva, made a vow to save all beings in hell. He is the only Bodhisattva in the whole Buddhist pantheon who is depicted as a monk; hence, his "shiny pate" or shaved head. The poet reminds us that hell is not an objective place that awaits us at the end of life, but hell is actually a state of mind carried around by each of us in our daily lives. Jizo's vow becomes our own resolve to spare ourselves from self condemnation.

Secret Buddha
Lurking in a cove,
Chiseled in the rock–
The homely face of love.

Buddhas appear in the most unlikely places.

Sitting uneasy
On an unfamiliar stone,
Huddled against the inevitable–
Seemingly alone.

When in the grip of fear or despair, the whole universe closes in. What was once seen as flowing and clear is now turbid and confused. The Zen student learns to treat such states of mind lightly—not adding to their weight by trying to figure them out. It would be like trying to get to the bottom of a rainy afternoon. Interior weather, like its meteorological counterpart, moves on.

Many distant mountains
Seen vaguely through the haze,
The Island of Immortals—
Beyond our worldly gaze.

Our various mythologies are there to
encourage and direct us. The mystical
Island of the Immortals, a kind of Taoist
heaven on earth, is nowhere to be found.
And yet, each of us is invited to establish
that "heaven" wherever we stand.

Lily pads hovering in the sun,
Other worlds float far from view,
Every place a Buddhaland—
But still "Namandabu."

Devotees of Amida Buddha constantly repeat his mantra so that when they die, they may be reborn in his Pure Land in the West. There are those, however, who know the Pure Land is already here and now. Yet even with nothing to attain, they still continue to repeat the mantra: Namu Amida Butsu.

When the mantra is repeated over and over, it begins to lose its consonantal edges, and the familiar formula becomes Namandabu—a rosary bead worn smooth.

At home in the ordinary,
Still they hear the music of heaven.
Playfully following both paths—
Free and easy wandering.

Chuang-Tzu calls this "walking two roads." The inner willingness to respond matches the outer world of constant transformation—nonchalantly meandering among the vicissitudes, floating along the waves of change.

Even when you're reeling from wine,
Or blazing with rage,
or shivering in fear,
There still is a place that
does not move—
Thirty spokes share an empty hub.

*The last line is from the eleventh
chapter of the Tao Te Ching in which
the image of a wheel is used to
emphasize that the whole whirling
world has, at its center, a place that is
still and empty.*

Among the ashes
Squats the new samurai,
Emulating the hidebound warriors
Of the old enemy.

Hiroshima, Ground Zero

Leaning on a stick,
The weary traveler stops to rest
along a stream,
Pausing for a moment—
A roaring current of stillness.

*All movement is relative. Is the old tree
the traveler or is it the stream? With all
this coming and going, where can we
find any rest?*

Look, a hundred and eight patriarchs
Jumping up and down on Temple Rock,
Kicking and cavorting, laughing
and shouting—
How can we escape this unbearable din?

If the mind is agitated, even the most
peaceful landscape becomes a scene of
confusion. When this happens, all efforts
to still the mind merely add to the clamor.
How can we escape this terrible hooha?
We can't. Just make your mind enormous.

Since Baso planted groves of trees
    For generations not yet born,
For all of those who came before–
    We gather here to mourn.

The story goes that, as an old man, Zen Master Baso was seen planting trees by one of his young disciples. The student inquired why he was doing this since the trees would not reach maturity for many decades. Baso replied that he was planting these trees for those who would follow. The Zen lineage founded by Baso was strong and lively, lasting a very long time. So each generation looks forward to the welfare of the those to come and looks backward to the ancestors, bowing in gratitude.

Hidden in the leaves,
The unblinking eye of the heron,
Watching for baby ducks–
Hail to the Bodhisattva of Compassion.

*This poem incorporates a pun on the
Chinese character "Kuan," which means
to watch or observe. This ideogram is
composed of two elements: heron and see.
The elements of the Chinese character
suggest a visual rhyme with eye, see,
heron, watching, and are also part of
the name of the Bodhisattva–Kuan Yin.
There is a feeling that even though the
heron is watching to pounce on any baby
ducks unlucky enough to happen by,
ironically the activity of Compassion is
present even here.*

Having descended into hell
And saved every tortured soul–
His work done for all time,
Jizo takes a well-deserved nap.

The Bodhisattva Kshitigarbha, known
as Jizo in Japan, has taken on the
consuming task of saving all beings
everywhere, but especially those
tormented in the fires of hell. The poet is
suggesting that beings are already saved
and only need to wake up to this fact–a
fact ironically made apparent by Jizo's
napping. The head of this statue was
damaged in the intense heat of the bomb
at Hiroshima. A visit to hell is not
without its risks.

Spring again,
The enthusiasm of the cherry blossoms,
But strangely—
There is never any fruit.

Every April, the cherry trees bloom in Japan. It is a festive time for everyone. Yet none of the several kinds of blooming trees actually bears fruit. Their only purpose is to bloom. In Zen, it is important to express one's life fully and openly without any special purpose in mind.

Battered Buddhas
Sitting on the tan,
Years and years of wearing away—
Roughness all but gone.

After years of sitting on the tan (the meditation platform in a monastery), successful monks tend to loosen their rigid views of who they are. They still have their unique personalities, but they no longer insist.

A householder has many things,
A monk has just a few—
But even a good thing
Isn't as good as nothing at all.

Having many things is wonderful; that goes without saying. Being able to restrict yourself to having only a few things is a great indulgence for which monks are appropriately grateful. The greatest indulgence of all, of course, is allowing yourself to have nothing. But so few of us can afford it.

Ancestor follows ancestor,
Endless cycles, descend and climb,
Joining the ancient procession—
One step at a time.

Overlooked and unusable,
This gnarled old tree,
Eluding the enterprise of busy minds–
Sprawls out its ancient calligraphy.

*Chuang-Tzu wrote about the bent and
twisted Shu tree that manages to
survive the ax because it is of no use to
anyone. Slowly and without concern, it
spreads out its lazy branches.*

Legs crossed, back straight,
Breathing soft and slow,
Rolling the Wheel one full turn—
I've never left my home.

Sitting in formal meditation, the breath turns slowly in a smooth, continuous cycle. Now we remember that we have never been away from home–that we carry this "home" with us always. The "Wheel" referred to is the Wheel of the Dharma. Turning the Wheel is accomplished on many levels–from the slow sweeping arc of a lifetime to the simple round of breathing in and out.